Family Album

Zoey

Jacob

Angelina

Mary

Jamie

Darren

Mary

Ian

Family Album

Poems
by Ian McDonald

Selected and edited
by Robin McDonald

ISBN 978-976-8244-58-1

 Design and layout by Paria Publishing Company Limited
www.pariapublishing.com

Typeset in MinionPro and Noto Serif
Printed by Lightningsource

Contents

Dedication IX
Acknowledgements XI
Introductory Poem XII

PART 1 - Ancestors **1**
Death Of An Old Woman (Mary's Grandparent) 2
Tears 7
Great Aunt Anna 8
Mount Pelée 10
The Golden Mast 11
Grandma's Story 13
The Wintry Road
   (For Barbara Callender – Mary's Mother) 14
Rug Of Fire 15
Lady With The Gold Parasol 16
Life Of Stones 17
Tea With Uncle Arthur 18

PART 2 - Parents **21**
Signalling 22
Beaucaillou 23
Concerning My Father And Mother 24
My Father's Prayer Book, Page 44 26
Father 27
The Red Crystal Necklace 29
Everywhere The Land Is Turning Green 31
Still Life 32
Tennis 33
The Sweet Lime Hedge 35

Red Stone Jar   36
Walking With My Father   37
Vanished Palaces   39
Anthuriums   40
Golden Oranges Of Esperanza   41
Sometimes I Hear The Rainfall Singing   42
Climbing   43
Star Taught   44
My Mother Sings Me Lullabies   45
Mother And Son   47
Mango Picking At One Carmody Road   48
Lullaby   49

PART 3 - MARY   **51**
Star of Love   52
Praise Song for Mary   54
How She Cuts The Bread   56
Of Course   58
A Good Thing   59
Masterpiece   60
A Useful Place   61
My Wife's Medical   62
The Golden Bangle   63
Perfection   64
African Violet   65
Again My Love I Need You   66
Her Tasks Done Well   68
I Know When I Am Dying   70
Forecast   71

PART 4 - Children   **73**
Life   74
My Son Selects A Stone   75
First Draft Of Unexplainable Love   76
Shadows Will Hide The Sun   77
The Face Of God   78

The Edge Of Things 79
That My Son Be Kept Safe 80
Kites, A Tiger Fang, A Golden Ring 83

PART 5 - Grandchildren **85**
Red Blossoms On A Moonlit Branch 86
The Old Age Of Plants 87
Jacob And The Moth 88
Poem For Zoey 89
The Truth About The Moon 90
The Grandchildren Enquire About My Death 91
Zoey's Cake 92
Shadows 93
"Again Again" 94
Measuring Heaven 95
Fun Day 96
Moon-Shadows 97
The Signal 98
Jacob 99
Zoey 100
Jacob's Tree 101
Time Is The Problem 102
Jacob's Question 103
Orchid Moon 104
Rampart With Red Flag 105
Angels Will Look After Him 106
Jacob Sums Up Time 107
A Sense Of Longing 108
Meeting My Grandson At School 109
The Grandchildren Tumble Me With Bright Pillows 110

About The Author 111
Books By Ian McDonald 112

VIII

To My Beloved Family

X

Acknowledgements

My thanks to:

Peepal Tree Press where many of these poems were first published.

My sister Robin who takes such care and helps so much.

Longtime and dear friend Clem Seecharan whose encouragement never fails me.

John Barnie whose poems and insights enlighten my life.

Alice Besson whose creativity as a book designer is unsurpassed.

Giselle Laronde-West who put the book together.

My wife Mary whose love is the indispensable inspiration.

Introductory Poem

Those we greatly love
deserve at least a rhyme
forget eternity
secure their place in time

I know very well
it will certainly be said
word-capturing is vain
what is dead is dead

enter these small markings
empty row on row
circumvent a little while
life's final zero

never seek to know
what's in all the forecasts
love all of you forever
while forever ever lasts

PART 1

Ancestors

Death Of An Old Woman

(Mary's Grandparent)

She was eighty-five. Death came for her
without fuss, walked in quietly,
nodded to us all and took her hand
as if to say, 'come now, it is time,
it will not be hard' - which she agreed
and lulled into the sleep that will not end.
She had been preparing, quiet came on her,
and then she wanted one last thing:
the summoning of a son she had not seen
for many, many years and wanted now to hold,
touch his face,remembering where that scar runs,
how he fell and cut a child's brow fifty years before.
She waited for that, his summoning, his tears,
put up her frail arms to be embraced,
sighed and touched his face again.
Wanting nothing more, she closed her eyes
and welcomed patient Death, the comforter.

With pride she'd kept the small and spotless house
she and her husband owned for fifty years;
when he died she followed old routines
that he had known and she would not forget.
In their corner room that catches the sea-wind
each morning, she cleaned floor and cupboards,
aired the clothes, made beds smooth and fresh,
always she must spend time at her window-sill
breathing in sea-wind and the smell of pomegranates,

looking out on what was her's and, further out,
far sky spreading and the sea, on what was God's.
This morning scene she knew by heart and loved
as men love things they make, like bread in their
own homes, earth daily dug, chairs and tables
not moved for generations
and seasons' chores that children teach their children.
The morning of the day she came to die
she could not reach the window from her bed,
asked those who waited there to carry her
again to breathe the salt sea-wind, that
all those fifty years smelled gentle, sweet,
and come next sunrise would not feel again.

As the day wore on, silence lengthened
in the air, and she got clear of things
at evening time when dark had not quite come
she died so soft one hardly knew,
and the stars shone brighter and the night went on.

She'd begged her sons that holy fire
should take her to eternal rest;
no dark and lonely earth should rot her bones,
or worms creep into flesh that once was sweet.
But fire! Fire she loved, the purity of fire.
'Entirely I am burned away,
I die and then I cease to die.'

She lay in white cloth, pure as light,
her white hair braided, limbs composed for sleep;
a husband-given bracelet from their courting days -
she loved this more than anything she owned -

hung on her fragile wrist, no other ornament
except clear lines of peace and beauty on her face.
Those she loved gathered where she lay,
they closed the casket at the last,
threw flowers in and fragrant herbs,
and heard the pandit speak the ancient words of hope:

'Life lasts a moment,
yet it does not end.
Even as a jewelled drop
returning to the sea
is this woman's life:
the sea is measurelessly deep;
even as a spark
from the great fire
is this woman's life:
the fire burns forever;
even as a single blossom
falling from the tree
in this woman's life:
the tree does not cease to bear.
Yesterday she was born,
tomorrow she is born again.
Entirely she is burned away;
the fire only mounts the higher.
If you shed tears
it is not for her they fall.
Does one sorrow for the boundless sea?
Does one sorrow for the great fire?
Does one sorrow for the blossoming tree?
Though darkness seems the lot of man,
all the universe is radiant light.'

We walked the enamelled fields of green -
ox-eyed flowers lined the way,
grasshoppers brushed against our feet -
and reached the place where she would burn
in brilliance in the flame she sought:
clear sky, oiled bier of wood, bright evening sun,
sea-wind to make the fire blaze and leap
heavenwards with the anointed soul.
There, on cleared ground, near the lapping waves,
we brought her, said the last farewells,
heaped aromatic wood around her like a house
where she would stay a moment, bathed in fire,
until the flames consumed her utterly,
even the bones made ash as light as petals.

At the far corners of the holy bier
Pandit directed where the sons should set the fire
slowly it caught the oiled wood, coiled, and grew;
soon flames were tall and climbing clear,
bright pennants in the evening air.
For her no sinking in dark earth
but a leap lightwards, a resurrection
made of burning light, the deepest caverns
of her soul made marvellously bright.
For an hour the clear flames leaped and soared,
then sank to glowing red, a flower in the night.

The chosen son walked lonely to the wall
at morning's flush of pear-pink light,
gathered the ashes in a blessed white cloth.
Fishermen took them on this journey
under a sky now bathed again in light,
and then he cast the ashes wide upon

the sacred bosom of the sea, and threw
a solitary flower from the garden
she had loved so well, and watched
it float far, far upon wave succeeding wave
until it too was lost in blinding light.

Tears

It's no good sobbing for the dead. They're gone,
they'll never be back. Do not expect that a visit
in your dreams will be the same thing as sweet life,
memories of love and laughter real again.
They won't return, they've left on their endless journey.
So no tears fall from the stone heart, better
so much better that grief be defeated.
Yet sometimes when the moon rises and the last
birds wing for home, I suddenly remember
and sob for those I loved and are gone.

Great Aunt Anna

my great-aunt Anna never married
they said she loved me her only son
every night she said her jewelled rosary
protect me so I never need to worry
I would be safe pass exams win the tennis
I went away didn't see her for years
the ceremony of blessing when I left was sad
she wrote me once her curving signature
she said her rosary I must not forget
every night and day I was not to worry
when I saw her at last she was far gone
"her mind has wandered from its moorings"
I went to visit don't know if she knew
her eyes blind in the quiet I sat
her old veined hand held mine tighter
tried to tell me something when she was young
when she was just a little girl she remembers
she climbed a tree deep into its green branches
and it was beautiful there in the green tree
and she was near to heaven

Great Aunt Anna's Gold Locket

Mount Pelée

Old beloved Aunt - I was the son she never had -
adored by her, she made me feel supreme;
she knew I would be a wonder of the ages.
I never ventured anything she did not bless.
She said the chaplet beads and rocked
in her chair of wickerwork and oak,
with prayers for victories in all I did.
Her gnarled and ancient hands, rosary-entwined,
told stories too by lamplight before sleep,
of how she lived in years gone by, how once
strange sunsets gleamed in the skies
of Port Of Spain for months, a blaze of crimson,
as if the sailing clouds were stained with blood.
She told me of the great volcano that blazed the doom
of forty thousand souls in Martinique's St. Pierre; how
The smoke of death arose and hung
a shroud around the sun
for months on end. It was so beautiful that arching sky
of blood, she never saw sunsets so red
and did not think of death.
Seventy years have flown. My great-aunt's chaplet
still winds protection around my adult years
and blood-red sunsets signify the sword of death.

The Golden Mast

at 84 Dundonald Street
grandma told me a story once
and only once she told it
a young boy went to sea
pretending to be a man
this was brave adventuring
he had found the way
ship's deck built of English oak
hull of strong pitch-pine
billowing sails of sturdy cloth
so finely was it made my child
it even had a golden mast
vessel fit for kings and queens
the good ship's maiden voyage
three days out of harbour-safety
storm blew the ship could not withstand it
waves roared higher than deck of English oak
soon breaks the hull of strong pitch-pine
the ship is sinking fast my child
the only hope the boy could see
the tall mast he could cling to
you know the story's end my child
gold sinks same as worthless stone.

Grandma's Story

Grandma did not tell us stories
she was too gentle for story-telling
story-tellers are strong and confident
they laugh and cry in their stories
so that you can laugh and cry
Grandma was not like that at all
but I remember one story she told very well
beyond the Northern Range of mountains
there was a little village tucked away
there was magic people good and true
fruit you picked from heavenly trees
and there were crystal springs of water
when you drank it took away all pain
why there doves even chased away the hawks
around that little village a rampart had been built
no evil could enter no sadness could come in
and within that rampart no one lived in vain
Grandma told the story many many times it was
Grandma's story I loved her telling it when I grew
older it made me very sad
I knew she told that story really for herself

The Wintry Road

(For Barbara Callender – Mary's Mother)

The family should prepare - come soon.
And so the sons and daughters came.
In bitter cold the roads are white,
they gleam like bone in winter light,
low horizon sun displays
bare, black-clawed silent trees.
Underfoot stone struck by boot
hard as chilled Antarctic ice;
bells ring silver in the frozen air
plead to save her in our chapel prayer.
So far from the hot-dust, donkey roads in Industry,
where, young, she walked to sell in morning markets,
weary hours in the brazen sun. She alone at work
for them - rent, food, clothes and books - for fatherless
years, counting the long years until they got the education
for which she yearned. On her deathbed now, from near
and far they gather and mourn, to thank and honour
she who created them and built good lives around
her sacrifice, families flourishing as she grew old.
Now snow hangs in the trees like dressings,
an extraordinary weight of silence
on the wintry road to her last resting place.
Ah what reaches the heart from the far stars,
to remind them forever of roughened hands
and tired eyes, night after night, when alone
she kept them safe from peril.

Rug Of Fire

silver-buttoned satin-suit and sunday best
hair trimmed and shiningly in place
first-born ready to be presented
grandest great-aunt in all the family
I would not want this to be lost
my mother and grandmother seriously instructed
the grand old lady I was prepped to meet
she was blind she would want to feel my face
and I was twice-told to kiss her cheek
dark and cluttered rooms to genuflect and whisper
what I remember best was quite another thing
beauty of the framed carpets on the wall
the rug I stepped on beneath her ancient chair
bright orange cloths woven into flames
like fire I thought as I stepped towards her
and I recall her sweet smile and embrace
not awkward at all bright fire at my feet

Lady With The Gold Parasol

old days in Port of Spain
tramcars round the Savannah
took you to the Gardens
where the bright birds flew
every Tuesday late afternoon
she passed by my grandmother
aunt Ivy gold parasol aloft
guarding milk white skin
far away empty eyes
beneath a light net veil
secrets failed men they said
brought little gifts for me
red toy soldiers sweets

Life Of Stones

sipped sherry from a crystal glass
fan she fanned with blue patterned butterfly
too old to be partying I thought
hunched back withered her
white hair beautifully coiffed though
"I have had a good hard life
the way was filled with stones
every stone became a jewel"
I have not forgotten

Tea With Uncle Arthur

so like my beloved father his young brother
short clipped grey abundant hair
how he stands slightly against the wind
crinkling lines about the eyes had seen Antiguan sun
their brothers' look steady clear and kindly
we went for tea and talk at the Copper Kettle
first term at Cambridge I was very young
had been asked I'm sure to check my settling in
for true I was not only young but a little lost
liked him very much at once and always afterwards
not for one moment stiff with fame at all
though he had made a mark upon the world
helped to beat Hitler in the great Battle of the Air
history will know him he would never tell
in the Copper Kettle we talked and laughed
he mentioned Hazlitt and found I knew him well
quoted him perhaps he had it planned and ready
"much thought on hard subjects after time
stems and dulls the dancing of the spirits
the gaiety of mind and weighs upon the heart
so making us disremember what we are about
enjoying every day's common sweet pursuits "
you must relish life without the lecture
if you have any trouble come to me
and even more if you have none at all
sudden familiar pang I recognize the smile

PART 2

Parents

Signalling

'After parties, in those courting days
He brought me safely to my door.
I could not bear to let him go,
Your handsome father - my young man,
He could not bear to leave me there :
When he left he turned and turned -
I see the stars above his head -
And tears of love came in my eyes.
A mile or so away he lived
Through trees, a tall apartment house:
We had a pact: when he got in
He lit a lamp, the window glowed,
He waved for me his silk-white scarf.
Heart raced to see that signalling.
My son, I feel my heart beat fast.'
The stars have burned for sixty years
The white scarf disappeared in dust.
My mother holds my father's hand;
Old and frail he sinks to rest.

Beaucaillou

The wind blows my mother's hair;
she speaks of Beaucaillou, her swift horse.
When she was a girl she recalls
the fine horse in his gleaming trap:
the snort and stamp and jingle
and her father laughing, clapping,
Shouting, 'Home, Beaucaillou, home!'
And the wind blowing in her red, wild hair.

Concerning My Father And Mother

never made a point of telling them
how much my parents meant to me
always treated me with love
praised me never put me down
discussed with me the doubts I had
backed me up when I decided
lost the first set in the final match
junior championship I set my heart on
from the stands my father signaled
and from then I knew I'd win
his and my mother's love -
no conditions were attached

respected everyone they dealt with
in turn bestowed the weight of benefit
their set example never failed us
in Antigua when they were very old
Cliff House home of such great beauty
sat in chairs sea-grapes in the wind
they talked with me a thousand memories
until a gold sky turned to night
then walked hand in hand towards the house
I followed up the shell-strewn path
thinking how much I always loved them
just then they turned as one and smiled
as if my voice had spoken to them
perhaps it did I write it now

My Father's Prayer Book, Page 44

Most life is ice-melt,
bells through sea-mist,
dark coming home and hurrying.
There are no exceptions.
Thoughtful men feeling
the stars' pull across half the world,
knowing coast's thick rocks
vanish in the seas' wash finally -
these men too have urgent private business:
they deal in golden things and lures.
Faded writing in a prayer-book's margin -
this remedy for love affairs and projects:
'Stand under old trees in the wind'.
Heaven is huge then and not temporary.

Father

he weakened in his final days
"too tired to listen to the radio
too tired" he smiled "to stay alive"
he rubbed his grey and stubbled face
said sorry that he couldn't shave
he who kept himself so well
I sit close and grasp his mottled hand
the liver spots have multiplied
my sadness makes it hard to breathe
calm grey eyes once steadied me
young and lithe on court and field
taught me so much I came to love
his love and confidence in me
meant nothing really could go wrong
way way back suddenly I see him
stride toward me with a bound of joy
takes and lifts me to the heavens high
soaring laughing – again! again! –
puts me down and hugs me hard
oh how I loved him then forever
forever my heart could burst
he asks me how I'm doing now
his free hand takes out a handkerchief
dabs the lids "not tears you know
just an old man's rheumy eyes"
wants me so bad to smile with him
"you have always made me proud"

the wind blows off the green-blue sea
as he has known for thirty years
"son get me up" I half-carry him
to look down on the beloved sea
where years ago we swam and sported
he leaned on me we watched together
where far far far far out the green and blue fades to
grey and then to nothingness

The Red Crystal Necklace

Blankness now, lips slightly agape,
vacancy of eyes that shone,
heavy length of body sags.
I sit beside her in despair.
She speaks of what was long ago,
asks for help to dab her eyes
with linen laid to wipe the tears.
The colours of the world are gone.

A portrait fixed above her bed
near seventy years ago
was her husband's favourite picture
of his bride. It shone for him
throughout their time.
As I look up her eyes catch mine.

The portrait is in black and white
necklace of black stars chained on glowing white.
She turns to give a lover's glance,
his heart forever stopped in wonder.

"It is as if it's happening now.
He asks me first to close my eyes,
places it round my bare neck gently
I feel them fall upon my breast,
red crystals with their weight of love.
I knew my world would end with him."
She sighs and slowly turns her face away.

Everywhere The Land Is Turning Green

"Well, eighty years to choose from, tell me quick -
don't think - the happiest moment of your life?"
My father's land, Antigua, our holiday home each year.
Antigua was like burnt bread, for two years drought
parched the land, water giving out everywhere,
the stone cisterns emptying in the house, boats
bringing water from Dominica. How long
could that go on? Whispers of an abandoned
island. Day after day sun blazed in an arc
of blue heat haze and smell of smoke. Perhaps
the cossi green would be all that's left -
a burned crisp in the ocean.

One morning black clouds piled, heavy storm-towers
in heaven. Pray, our parents said, pray, pray.
When the rain came hard on the roof, I went out
with my small sisters. Yes, you go, our parents said.
We danced wild dances in the rain - what would
have been forbidden - we danced and laughed again.
Our parents came and we were lifted up.
Next day the rain came hard again, everywhere
the land turning green.

Still Life

My father ran estates in Trinidad,
open trays of coffee drying in the sun.
Green gold grapefruit cannon balls
fell in high wind on the high roof
of low, unpainted agricultural sheds -
scents and sounds of childhood never lost.
I see wood choppers bend,
cutting cocoa wood in sweaty vests.
I see a big man wave and shout.
The boys gone on a parrot hunt!
The overseer lifts me on his shoulder
to get ripe governor plums from high.
Shadow of rainfall in the far hills.
How do such images last forever?
The coffee beans are fragrant still;
the gold-green grapefruit fall and clang;
I reach up high for purple plums.

Tennis

Feeling the joy of immortal youth,
being healthy and wanting to run, leap,
feel fresh air and golden sun scorch
face and back, on afternoons of dark clouds
gathering, I prayed rain would stay away
so tennis could be played. I would
get faster, better, stronger, fitter,
getting the body ready to win.
I pounded the ball against a wooden wall,
until the rhythm entered me, hour
after hour until dizzy I almost fell.

I risked sunstroke, my mother scolded.
Too much of a good thing. Go and rest.
She sopped my head, kissed and hugged me
with a worried look. Once I found
blister blood, hid the socks from her.
My father told me when alone, Get a hat, son.
Apply sunscreen, take a jug of sweetened lemonade.
Gradually I got better hitting at the wall,
never lonely - the game was my companion.
Then getting on the competition ladder -
first time I knew I would be good, hit a backhand
volley with perfect timing, to the inch I aimed at,
against Darnley Scandella, a good strong journeyman
whom I never beat and now I beat him easily.
He praised me and took my hand in his.
Such a delight to feel the body muscling up,
movements swifter, reflexes sharp, balance more assured,
breathing after hard running, easier and easier,
heart coming to rest so quickly after exertion;
how to make the right shots embedded in the brain.
Felt invincible, marched to inner exultation;
days were not long enough to contain the victories.
Once I saw a tiger lash its tail - that was me.
When I think of being young, fit, striving
with the flourish of good health, mind desiring
rivalry and winning, ready for glory
on the courts and honouring the body trained
in a sort of perfection - well, all this,
I think, is to describe happiness.

The Sweet Lime Hedge

over all the sweet lime hedge
butterflies flew when I was young
came down from Benedictine hills
lit by the gold of poui trees
they were so many I remember
I ran among them as a child
arms outstretched to gather them
falling multi-coloured leaves
laughed with joy they brushed my face
my mother came to join me once
laughing joyfully as I did
picked me up hugged and kissed me
I knew I was blessed then
I knew I was blessed forever

Red Stone Jar

80 years ago vivid still as swallow
it stands so well so strongly fashioned
our mother kept it near the pantry door
a shelf with biscuits and slab of cheddar cheese
stone jar made water cooler without ice
when we dashed in from playing in the sun
poured the water from the red stone jar
and to myself said ah that's good
our mother there she mopped my head
gave me a kiss don't get sunstroke now
the cool fragrant taste of water
our mother the red stone jar and love

Walking With My Father

my father wakes me before the sun comes up
climb down the little shell-strewn beach
below the cliff we stayed for holiday
where sea-scented winds blessed us all day long
walked along the coast waves around our feet
sometimes saw sun rise marvelously blood-red
amid black horizon clouds glowing veins of gold
sometimes fishermen passed with lobster pots

my father bargained with them if the catch was fresh
he talked with me so much and again much more
whatever caught his fancy more than that I'm sure
puzzling and strange never found it boring
eleven years of age my mind easily caught fire
war and peace life and death everything in between
invading Nazi Europe excitement in his voice
what it meant history's sweep spent some time explaining
my father was a quiet man but he could tell a story
years have lengthened into lives since we walked together
remember how he thrilled to tell the storming of the
beaches
cricket heroes books to read why I hated maths
sugar factory where he worked years alone in England
cocoa plant research he'd done at the Imperial College
doctor Grandpa's surgery the poems Grandma wrote
I had much more to say as the walks continued
he listened well so I found our talks became adventure
and often such splendours in our walks occurred
beauty of the morning sky changing colours of the sea
moments of nature's thousand gifts how could I forget
albatross soars along the heights of heaven exulting
from him I came to sense the wonders of creation
a best time of my life I knew from ever since
those walks along Antigua's coast my father long ago
and it is good to tell the joy of coming back
find my mother's breakfast feast waiting on the table
fried chub cutlets fungi cakes scrambled eggs just so

Vanished Palaces

in the museum when I was a seeking boy
strange wondrous astonishments looked down
first visit to this keeper of history and adventure
took my father's hand in curious quiet rooms
images of tapestries armour goblets and old bibles
abounded and enthralled me that marvelous world
palaces have vanished into dust my father said
one thing I remember exactly a vivid treasure
ancient Persian sword scabbard scrolled in gold
to this hour I recall the swirling red inscription
"this sword killed a king and set a princess free"
centuries of wonder blazed and never left me

Anthuriums

my mother put down red anthuriums
in rich black soil beneath the great samaan
she loved the work of gardening the joy
recall that day a setting sun
blush of red in heaven's clouds
she had her basket from the Rapsey farm
vivid leaves of emerald plants
"son come help me plant anthuriums"
ah that time that sweet boyhood time
the care and love my mother showed
blood-red anthuriums beneath the great samaan

Golden Oranges Of Esperanza

showed me with pride the golden oranges
in mounds for collection at Esperanza
the best of all our fruit he said
plant with care manure bring to perfection
uncrowded rows well tended truly kept
nothing better than the earth made fruitful
when crops were good I saw my father's joy
at the Union Club no doubt it was the money
the way he told me it was something more

Sometimes I Hear The Rainfall Singing

sometimes I heard the rainfall singing
but it was not the rain it was my mother
in the room next to mine rain and my mother
at her needlework or fixing the baby's clothes
making up her cot everything done with love
everything my mother did she did with love
she would sing with such a sense of happiness
why I found the rain's voice comforting
all my boyhood it was my mother singing

Climbing

When I was a daring boy
trying things on the bike
rushing into the waves
my mother hugged me hard,
said, Look before you leap.
My father taught me about climbing trees:
Test the branches are strong enough -
Experiment on one, holding another.
Slip - you can still hold on.
He showed me how in the big orange tree.
I think of them now so long ago.
Always had fall-back.

Star Taught

My father liked to show me stars
on clear nights, pointed out Orion,
his gold belt and sharpened sword,
silver cluster of the Pléiades safe forever
from the Boethian hunter; and, from the veranda
of our parents' room, the North Star shining
over Mount St. Benedict. Pictures in the night,
he drew for me of glory, bravery and myth,
the abiding beauty of the steadfast star.

My Mother Sings Me Lullabies

pain seized me I cried out in horror
eighty years gone his gold watch is still swinging
rotund Dr. Littlepage whispers I will die
unless I get to hospital he will call the surgeon
woke from blackness after they had stifled me
white-coated torturers tore me from my parents
the cracked ice shone like diamond chips
silver spoon my mother placed against my lips
tears glistened in her eyes like diamonds too I saw
she brought mercy to me in my raging thirst
I cried and cried for her she never left my side
no visitors at night her anger struck them down
"you tie me up with ropes I will still come in"
beloved mother such fierce beauty I have never known
I knew then all my life I would be safe forever

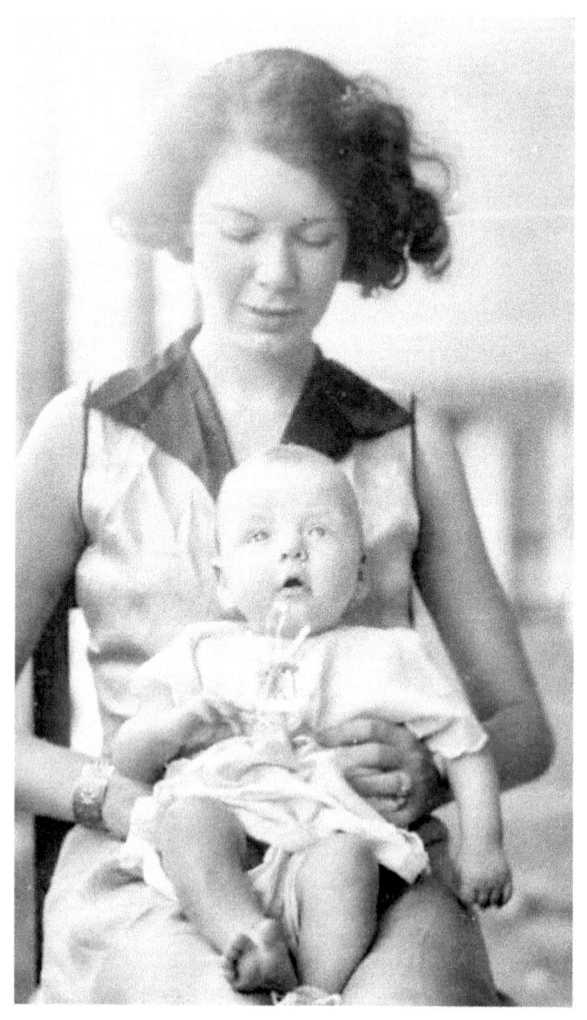

Mother And Son

from dusty storage in Antigua
I hold a portrait just as old as me
now closing in on eighty-six
hardly believe how beautiful and young
she looks cradling the first-born in her arms
smile of love and triumph in her eyes
head tilted as I at once recalled
my ancient heart hurting to remember
the confidence and love she made a part of me
tears sting though I resist them
young mothers never think
of sons grown old and dying

Mango Picking At
One Carmody Road

the winds of life have blown the years away
our lovely St. Augustine home vanished long ago
happiest of families lived the happiest of times
who can deny what none of us will doubt
tears fall to think that not a trace remains
but now and then moments come in dreams
my father and my mother in the upper garden
he climbs a laden mango tree look out
throws down ripe fruit my mother does not catch
he laughs and she complains with such a lovely look
her beauty catches at my heart the love
between them gave certainty in all our lives
"you need to practise catching love" he says
"oh you just don't throw them properly"
he drops down from the tree they hug and laugh
the dream dissolves but when I wake they live

Lullaby

song sings in memory
forever and one day
fog blowing from the river
stepped on mossy rocks
slid to the very edge
danger far below
the moon lurched
tumbling gold saucer
when my cradle capsized
my mother caught me
quicksilver heart and hand
she steadied me
safe across all those years

PART 3

Mary

Star of Love

("At this time of year in the early hours of the morning
Venus can be seen at its brightest in the eastern sky" -
1988 Almanack - the sky at night for December)

My son cries out
and I am up to see him.
The sky is dark,
sea-wind blows in the rain;
there it blazes in the Eastern heavens,
the star of Love riding in the clouds alone,
gold ember burning tiger-bright.
Memory flies back
when I too was young:
my mother pointing
when I woke in tears,
voice gentle as a shepherd's flute:
'That is Christ's star,
Star of love, my son.
It brings beauty to the earth,
blesses all of us.'
Now as I comfort him
I point again to the great star
blazing in the Eastern heavens;
my son looks in a wonder
that dries the tears in him.
And through the night is dark
and the hard rain blows in

my heart is filled again
with hope, the promise
that has lasted centuries.
'What is it?' My wife whispers,
our new child heavy in her.
'The Star of Love,' I say
'The Christmas Star, my love'

Praise Song for Mary

Rounded
O of love
boon of heaven
heavy-looking now
birth soon to come
I celebrate the joy
beauty of body-swell
oval paradisal
proud miracle
I celebrate
all soft and circling forms
earth-root flower
the golden pregnant moon
showers shadows
call-glory of carols
bowls of ripe oranges
rose mangoes full plums too
stuffed sweet melons
rotund sun-ball in the sky
fat cloud-bellies sailing
in looms and loops of light
smoke-mist over water
rain curves on river
ocean-swoops billows
roses pools of moon-water
home home home
hollows look hallowed

they are the kin of hoops
fat loaves -
hot bounty
from old stoves
noontime and swallows
arcs of light
you are buoyant with becoming
a fountain
a meteor shower
flower-bloom
my burgeoning love
rock and cradling stars
in your belly-dark
time booms
and throbs and towers
life starts again
I hear the double-heart
that God made with me
and you will make me soon
a high-shining son.

How She Cuts The Bread

I see her cutting the bread
carefully in slices all about the same
puts the pieces in the toaster
turns to prepare big cups of Cappuccino
the bread out of the toaster buttered
she puts on the Cheddar cheese I like
gets froth on the Cappuccino right
how I like to see all this done
and that is not all by any means
she cuts the oranges peels the tangerines
sometimes I like to help in this
set the morning table that's my job
for years I've set it perfectly for two
the crystal glasses catch the sun
she could not live without flowers
that I learned from her and loved
flowers always everywhere amid green
yellow buttercups spider orchids red ixora
tangled in green fern in ceramic bowls
Amerindian universe patterned on their sides
and so she brings a garden into where we live
windows thrown open the sun also comes in
the table set with food peaceful comfort of the day
we talk of everything grandchildren in particular
the usual news how quickly they grow up
but not so quick they do not hurry to our arms
laugh-lament over mishaps of our gardener

beloved Kenneth thirty years watched over his domain
we try to understand the world so ill-reported
but what's the use we do what good we can
this is a place of unequalled treasured peace
the simple act of sitting down to eat and talk
sacramental what other word is there
when ritual is enriched with exchange of love
blessed this way the day has started well.

Of Course

a friend is coming soon
show us his red macaw
Mary has sliced green mangoes
so good with salt and pepper
in the shadow of a rainbow
the children are dancing

A Good Thing

thinking of the good things in life
not the grand things the exciting things
the headlines the highlights the heaven-sent
not the silver fire of an Essequibo moon
looking at my wife making up our bed this morning
carefully she unfolds the linen sheets
smooths them again again to perfection
making sure they fall evenly over the sides
plumps the pillows in flowered cases
takes a look making sure the final checks of love
how long have I known her life itself
I catch a hint of fragrance in the room

Masterpiece

Today mid-morning in Mary's kitchen,
all the ingredients branch of red cherries,
lettuce on a plate, wedge of yellow cheese,
shoulder of lamb, cutting board with bread,
jug of cold water, and lady in a flowered apron;
all it needs now is Matisse

A Useful Place

in Mary's bustling kitchen
vegetables simmering in a pot
basil celery on the cutting board
iced drink refreshes from the lemon tree
bless what the useful garden grows

My Wife's Medical

scanned her from top to toe
all well I could have told them so
then she's flawless? - no
full of temperament I know
and apt to find me wanting though
rock steady when the rough winds blow
a rare gift hers the Gods bestow
in barren soil she makes things grow
heaven whence hopes no longer flow
and bitter cold the earth below
her life is fire I love the glow

The Golden Bangle

one morning gathering spices
she thought she lost her golden bangle
we searched in nearby nettle beds
breathed deep no good I smiled
unlike your lovely herbs my love
gold has no smell at all

Perfection

look out on the orchids
profusion so precise
purple white on green bamboo frames
she takes such meticulous care
fixing them ordering them
canopy of perfected colour
don't take this for granted

African Violet

my wife has put beside my desk a lovely flowering plant
African Violet nestled in an emerald hand-made pot
stands out against white curtains catching gusts of wind
could not do without it now reminds me of love
consoles me affirms so many things good in life
five violet buds this morning emerge amidst the green
gift of jewels entangled within the heart-shaped leaves
just to my left I can touch them if I put down my pen
every day she waters this treasured plant she chose
look she is precisely careful not overmuch enough
smiles exchanged we know it will last forever

Again My Love I Need You

years and years and years we shared together
full-blossomed the garden of our life
sky's grey emptiness now deeply saddens me
day-long dark choir of the mourning trees
grown old towards the endless end of time
shivered in the night my dearest one
heart clutched by cold consuming fear
grasped your sleeping hand my love
ah life work-roughened ember-warm to touch
you murmur in your sleep my love
I find again the truth of love
stay with me beyond the shadows
until bright birds of morning sing

Her Tasks Done Well

she goes downstairs to gather flowers in the sun
she does not see that I am seeing her
such a lovely thing my world is calmed
slowly she goes from bed to bed getting flowers
choosing them carefully for colour and for beauty
humming to herself brushing back her hair
and now she bends and digs out tough weeds
puts them in a special bag for garden rubbish
ah look she screens her eyes to watch the parrots fly
she goes over to the herb beds growing separately
looking I see she has the scent of them
I myself can almost smell them breathing deeply
how good this is watching her in the flowers
digging out the tough weeds smelling the herbs
with separate baskets for flowers and herbs
then she sits in the shade of the Orchid House
a while she rests wind in the trees above her
she doesn't stay long she is always hard-working
her mother told her day after day never waste time
she is happy with what she has done I can see
wanting to come up fix the flowers pack the herbs
I'll greet her with golden apple juice well chilled
share some time look at the beauty of the flowers
she will not know how completely content I am
to have seen her pick the flowers gather the herbs
sit by herself a little while quiet looking happy
her tasks done well good things for those she loves
I do not think it matters how old the universe will ever be

I Know When I Am Dying

I know when I am dying
I will praise the beauty I have known
the blessings of the passing days
the wonder the heaven-spray of stars
I know when I am dying
I will praise the travelled world
the sun dawning on strange mountains
the moon racing in wild storms
the surging stallions of the sea
I will praise the glorious cities
where I found so many friends
I will praise the infinite store
of all the wisdom I have touched
the truths I tried so hard to learn
I will praise the kindness shown me
bravery against power that is hard
I will praise those who helped the poor
I will praise the children
their joy in life has fulfilled me
may their days shine forever
as my days have shone for me
I will praise the great river
we swam there that first morning
you sleek as a seal eyes shining
welcoming me into your arms
above all I know my heart
I know when I am dying
I will praise you my dearest
I will praise your love

Forecast

we are not what we fear we will become
not yet anyway not sad not sick not nothing
I have risen with birdsong strong and healthy
"for my age" as old men proudly claim
you have arranged the flowers made the coffee
we sit and talk about the day to come
old Cameron the gardener will bring his gold papaws
tell us about his harvest with pleasure in his voice
we know the grand-children are visiting a great blessing
exchanging stories about them we laugh into each others' eyes
it's hard but we avoid the hate in headlines
there are so many ways to love this world
the time immediately ahead of us is very good
outside we will walk amidst the red blaze of poinsettias
there is the music of the wind in the tall trees
let me say the earth is giving a good account of itself
today and tomorrow and as long as we want to think
we can forget completely what the old priest's sermon said
all beauty raised on high will also be thrown down

PART 4

Children

Life

I had two daughters born
each one lived a single day
I have lived ninety years
still sometimes I wonder
did my little girls before they died
know what life was meant to be
flash of wonder they could never be
the nothing of never having been
did they feel the presence of desire
to be and know what being is
do not be absurd the science says
I've been told and have learned by heart
yet my thinking has no end
in the small eternity they lived
did they feel the desperate wave of love
which should have saved them
as long long ago they passed this way?

My Son Selects A Stone

When he was six I was fifty-six
all that week-long holiday
my son brought stones from the sea.
What is this? A shark's tooth from the deep.
And these? Leaf of whitened coral.
Wave-worn bottle once held pirate rum.
Crystal from a drowned sailor's chain.
Magenta tile broken from a Great House floor,
a gleam of porcelain treasure-cup
snippet of glinting quartz we long pored over.
Are these valuable diamonds, Dad?
He lined them up to show his mother. Proud
cornucopia from the eternal sea. She praised him.
At the end he threw them all away,
kept none of the beautiful, curious,
the sea-shaped wonders he had found
and brought for our appraisal,
but kept a solid, ordinary, small rock
no different from a scattered multitude
that I could see. He has it still.
He never told us why he kept it

First Draft Of
Unexplainable Love

when your mother brought you home
I held you in the cup of my hand
along my forearm balancing you
completely helpless minute perfect fingers clenched
your heart must have been a pebble's size
but it did its job thank God of Gods
as well I thought as whatever mighty engine
keeps the universe going through all eternity
how I felt a surge of unimagined love
I will defend you against death and hurt forever
your eyes opened caught mine in joy and gratitude
nothing would ever mean as much again

Shadows Will Hide The Sun

(For Darren, at the Ceremony of Baptism)

Bathe him in light
I pray, bathe my son in light:
his be a good life's lustre.
Through a world growing dark
every passing hour
bathe him in light.
Let brightness gleam about him;
bitter will be days to come,
shadows will hide the sun.
Thus is the life of man,
but within him let brightness dwell.
Spare him dullness all his days,
defend him ever from despair.
From valley depths
let Heaven lead him;
never lose the mountain light.
Through gall and ash
a pearl will shine:
let his life gleam.
In the dark world
bathe him in light.

The Face Of God

Will we see God one day? He asked,
my beloved son when he was a boy.
I'd educate him solemnly and smartly,
I thought, tell him how God
was in all the beauty of the world,
in sunset clouds, the moon that rises,
crashing ocean waves, the creatures of the world.
I gestured - He's in all of us.
Look at those orchard plums ripened by God!
I impressed myself with the point I'd made.
He didn't seem very interested,
soon went away to play with friends.
Now I am old I see he meant his meaning -
no nice distractions - I want to know myself.

The Edge Of Things

Children love edges, should they see a cliff
they climb to see what depths are, watch them
in their beds, they roll towards the margins
ready to fall, to find out. They incline to where
mysteries are, they crave the discovery of ends,
not fearing to fall into the unknown.
Older they grow cautious. See them thinking twice.
They slow down near precipices, observe
boundaries, limit themselves to the middle ground,
to solid footing, the outcome calculated.
Strange, now I am old the urge to begin anew -
adventure in high places of the mind,
risking, little knowing. Soon I will
fall over the edge of everything

That My Son Be Kept Safe

My small son burns with fever,
his whole body is furnace hot,
burning to death he seems.
"I'm so sick Dad", he'd said
his eyes beseeching me to help.
Now his eyes are closed,
his dark lashes long like mine they say.
His breath rasps hard and dry;
it is agony to hear it.
To touch his brow stops my heart.
The doctor, stone-faced, stern-browed –
though we try to catch a saving glance –
will not look us in the eyes.
My wife smoothing the bed, doing anything,
anything to help, to keep busy,
trembles with fear. I tremble equally.
It is the worst fear in the world,
fear of a sadness beyond all sadness:
God forbid this should befall.
All the years that pass
would not cancel out the hour.
Why are we constructed so?
were it not better to be a stone?
I remember times we watched him,
coming to his bed because we could not hear his breathing,
bending low and lower to catch the breath
just raising the small chest.

The slightest twitch of coverlet or ribbon
showing he was safe among the smothering pillows
was most sweet, most easing
of this fear we all have always
that they will die and leave us.
No hope at all, the rest of life made senseless,
no ransom can ever meet this threat.
He burns to death
and my whole self cries to heaven.
For him to keep safe I would vow it now
to be good in God's sight always, always;
good father, good husband, good man,
Christ's good soldier even.
Though rum's still sweet
and friendship's fine, and laughter,
and a girl's walk catches the groin
and the world is so beautiful
and the wonder of every minute never ceases
I would give it all away forever
to let his eyes not close, my God,
that my son be kept safe.
And if God will not listen,
if God stops his ears,
so that small son be saved,
I would make a pact
with the hobgoblin in Hell
who loves sudden misery,
who strikes when life is most fit,
To give all my gold,
give blood-health, body-tune, eyesight,
the touch of wind and water that I love,
memories I have of tender hours,
reason that controls all things

the life God gave me,
the immortal soul,
I would give away
should my son be safe now;
safe now, my God, my God!

Kites, A Tiger Fang, A Golden Ring

Morning broke clear across the sky,
water gleamed amidst the green glades.
A glorious chorus
of sweet birds sang.
I hugged my wife
and the children slept in safety.
Later we put up the kites
to sing in the high wind
across the sun.
With shouts of fear and excitement
the children found a tiger's fang
near the old engineer's tomb,
a giant tooth-claw on a bone.
I picked it up and told fearful tales
of the wild forest and the night.
When the stars appeared –
a black castle of such dazzling lights! –
my son and I sat under the sky
discussing mysteries.
Later, showering in lamplight,
my gold ring gleamed
- my grandmother's when I was young –
and I thought how it might end.
How long does gold last?
How long are rings kept?
Lost? Given to a careful son?
Sold if it comes to that?
Or on my bright bone still
In endless night?

PART 5

Grandchildren

Red Blossoms On A Moonlit Branch

what are you doing Granddad you look sad
not sad my Zoey I am just concentrating
is concentration sad it seems to me it is
not sad really I'm trying to write a poem
it isn't coming out right at all that's sad
well Granddad I think maybe I can help you
my brother and me were writing poems too
we made a list what to write I can lend you
lovely Zoey that's lovely please let me see
I will Grandad when I get home I'll look
but now I remember one Jacob wrote I loved

The Old Age Of Plants

one time my grandson asked
how can you tell a plant is old
it looks a darker green I said
I didn't really know of course
but recall I told him once
come to me whenever ever
I know everything to know

Jacob And The Moth

why do moths try to kill themselves
flying round the lamp my grandson asks
Jacob it is not death they seek
it is their sun they want to reach
life would be worth it if they could
but they would die if they succeed
that is true we must think about it
do we prefer to live or dying reach the sun
well I'd prefer to live and just look at the sun
sensible I have to say Jacob you are right
ah what great cause I smile and think
may one day come to claim him

Poem For Zoey

I found a flower like a flame
it leaped skywards to be free
fire at the heart of beauty
blazes now for all to see

The Truth About The Moon

when my grandson was three
will the moon go out granddad
no it has a job to do
the lantern of the moon
guides home the white heron

The Grandchildren Enquire About My Death

of course I will still be around
I love you very much always will
those who love you always stay around
somewhere you can be sure of that
happy or sad or good or bad or medium
I'm going to be taking a big interest in you
remember I'll still be in the universe you know that
no part of the universe ever dies ever
all the time you are growing up getting old even
I'll be around keeping an eye on both of you
the important thing is I love you very much
so I'll be around you can be very sure
things like hugging me around my neck
or running away faster than I can catch you
you may not be doing these things that's true
but you know very well something important
what you think and feel inside you every day
means as much as what you do outside of you
and inside you is where you will always find me
everything will be well don't worry yourselves
now come and hug me tight around my neck

Zoey's Cake

relaxed reading about Gauguin and Van Gogh
in sun-drenched Arles creating masterpieces
steps away Zoey helps her grandmother
in the kitchen baking Zoey just aged six
jumping up and down wanting so much to help
of course you can do this do that
such excitement my beloved little granddaughter
climbing on the kitchen stool laughing with joy
her hand held to guide the electric mixer
and then the first sweet drops of essence in the mix
helped her hold the wooden spoon to stir
couldn't help smiling to see the happiness
the jumping the laughing that pure delight
put on this baking apron we're doing icing now
all the little sprinkles grandma the silver and the gold
yes my love we won't forget the silver and the gold
we're doing well Zoey this will be very good
my wife hugging her on the tall kitchen stool
Zoey laughing sheer dancing joy I'm helping
is it going to be the best best cake Grandma
it's going to be the best best cake anyone ever made
Zoey you helped me you truly helped me
her laughter and the dance for joy it lasts forever
I have lived a long life and I have known delight
left it very late to know this joyous perfect moment

Shadows

in and out the sun
walking once with Jacob
"Grandad, are shadows real?"
"let's kick one and see!"
did so vigourously to show
"but, Jacob, that's not all"

"Again Again"

I swing my little granddaughter in the sun
a golden day trees sounding like the sea
remember how I swung my young son high and happy
no dancing hair of such gleaming beauty
but that laugh of joy and love again again I hear
whole decades pass and it is yestermorning
will she ever know why she is hugged so tight

Measuring Heaven

how tall is heaven my grandson asks
I look up at the towering blue and smile
well I heard that on the tallest mountain
there is the tallest tree with one shining branch
if you climb there you can touch
not very tall then Jacob said matter of fact

Fun Day

the children run in laughing
waving flags gold white and green
Zoey held a red one aloft
they were so clearly happy
then what's this all about
well Granddad the teachers said
we just would have a day of fun
no lessons just the fun they said
Well okay you're sure I said

Moon-Shadows

are moon-shadows the same
as the sunlight makes he asks
Jacob walking with me in the garden
great globe of the full moon shining
they are the shadows of a ghost
sun's a magician with golden clothes
he has emerald-coloured eyes
those shadows gleam with heaven's light
he smiles with alarm and love

The Signal

Jacob says he has a sign
a signal he will send
I wave from the veranda
he signals from the Orchid House
shapes the hand-heart well

Jacob

Today he wants to know about whales.
He saw a Great Blue on a TV programme,
their hearts as big as limousines.
In his third year of life's astonishments,
wonder is everything. What is the circling moon,
flowers, the quickest bird, why hummingbird?
What is that on my desk? It's my Kaieteur stone.
Easy replying when what is there is simply there.
What is blood, how rain falls from heaven
are possible to explain. The darkness of night,
swords and castles, how fires burn – easy.
Beloved grandson, you will not stop there long.
It won't be only how planes stay in the sky,
how we breathe air into our beating hearts,
It will get harder. I must prepare myself.
It will not be long before you want to learn
what is fear and pain and cruelty and age.
Why death will be the hardest one of all –
to tell the truth but soothe his heart.

Zoey

my granddaughter
laughs in the garden
better than bird-song

Jacob's Tree

in the good earth
planted an almond
sixty years to come
under green branches
my grandson reads a poem

Time Is The Problem

hawks hang in the blue air
in their green frames purple orchids bloom
Zoey is painting moonlight and sunsets
on the green lawn the laughter of young men
take notice

Jacob's Question

Where am I in me? my grandson asks.
At six he's serious, he has worked it out,
the question, not the answer, clear.
I say the me is all of you that wants
to be attended to. It tells me when
to laugh or cry, tells me when to love or hate.
Where is I? Let's make a start.
I think it is the centre of the heart.

Orchid Moon

walked out to see moon-shadows
strange brightness strong and clear
restless birds are singing very late
orchid light I've heard it called
why unless orchids are rare
Jacob in his learned way commented
"day has left some sun behind"

Rampart With Red Flag

on the balcony of the forest house
river stretching like the sea
my grandson on the tropic beach
(how easily I see sand slips between his fingers)
builds elaborate castles in a row
studiously defended with well-shaped walls of sand
on each he puts a green leaf for a flag
hurries to finish as the tide comes in
red leaf tops the last and strongest rampart
as the first small wave laps against the wall
he seems satisfied - waves

Angels Will Look After Him

walking with nine-year Jacob evening sun aflame
along the Seawall where it first was built
it was good talking why the wall was there
look how the land is far beneath our feet
and the vastness of the sea was another subject
what we know is just a thimble of the ocean
then afar an old man I could see was crazy
strode towards us blood-glaze in his staring eyes
gestured to the sun lips opened in a roar
oh sun blaze fury-red before the day is done
exactly that he uttered how could I forget
put Jacob the safe side of me as the old man passed
close up he seemed to have devoured stones
his mouth agape you saw the bloodied gums
quietly he passed us not a sign of rage
my grandson silent then he said to me
"I am sad for that old man he looks so bad
he has no teeth Granddad what will happen now"?
"angels will look after him" held him to my heart

Jacob Sums Up Time

before my grandson tells me
is what now once was
after is what it's going to be
so now is all we have Grandad
forever and forever I laugh so easy
for him to say these things
soon he'll get to know
some of his life is in the past
the rest is in the future

A Sense Of Longing

life is so short
I write this in my 90th year
I say this for a reason
all of today has been a rare occurrence
the sun slanting through the window
glistening on the African violets
I've been sent brilliant vivid pictures
butterflies caught on the hills of Mount St. Benedict
hunted amidst the poui trees in my boyhood
my wife has made me an omelette
cheese and chopped mushrooms
I've never tasted even routines can be new
looked in the mirror combed my hair differently
the grandchildren are clattering up the stairs
look look what we found
what is it whatever it is is happiness
and the day is not even a quarter over

Meeting My Grandson At School

When children see who come for them,
who knows how far the reach of heaven goes?
Smiles light their faces and those who meet them
light with love and pride. Such reciprocities
bring tears to my eyes as I see again and again
pure love in my land. Jacob, a little late, sees me,
gives a little leap, waves shyly with his serious-sol-
emn smile, runs into my open, universal arms.

The Grandchildren Tumble Me With Bright Pillows

the grandchildren are joyous around me
they laugh play tickle my neck
last night silence lay in wait
except one harsh sound of a night bird
frightening me making me think of death
after all this time after so much life
a thin moon sailing in a black sky
was not beautiful a scudding storm of rain
came soon afterwards shaking my home my heart
generations vanish like the morning dew
but now the grandchildren are joyous around me
they tumble me with bright pillows

About The Author

Born in 1933 in St. Augustine, Trinidad, son of Archie and Thelma McDonald née Seheult. Educated at Queen's Royal College in Port of Spain and Cambridge University where he took an Honours Degree in History. Lived and worked since 1955 in Guyana where he became Director of Marketing and Administration in the Guyana Sugar Industry and CEO of the Sugar Association of the Caribbean. Played at Wimbledon in the 1950s and captained Cambridge and then Guyana at lawn tennis and subsequently the West Indies Davis Cup Team in the 1960s. Author of *The Hummingbird Tree* and 12 books of poetry and won the Guyana Prize of Literature in 1992, 2002, 2012 and 2023. Editorial Assistant to the Sridath Ramphal West Indian Commission in 1991/92. Member of the P.J. Patterson Committee on the Governance of West Indian Cricket in 2007/08. Chairman of the *Stabroek News* 2009–2021 and has written a weekly column for the newspaper for 40 years. Awarded Guyana Golden Arrow of Achievement 1986. Honorary Doctorate of Letters from UWI, St. Augustine in 1997. Fellow of the Royal Society of Literature since 1970. Married to Mary Callender with sons Jamie and Darren and a son Keith from a previous marriage.

"Antiguan by ancestry, Trinidadian by birth, Guyanese by adoption, West Indian by conviction".

Books By Ian McDonald

Fiction
The Hummingbird Tree (1969)

Poetry
Selection – Faber: Poetry Introduction 3 (1975)
Mercy Ward (1988)
Essequibo (1992)
Jaffo The Calypsonian (1994)
Between Silence And Silence (2003)
The Comfort Of All Things (2012)
River Dancer (2016)
New And Collected Poems (2018)
People Of Guyana (with Peter Jailail, 2018)
Poems For Mary (2020)
The Garden (2021)
Not Quite Without a Moon (2023)

Drama
Tramping Man (1969)

Non-Fiction
Cloud Of Witnesses (2012)
A Love Of Poetry (2013)
An Abounding Joy – Essays on Sport
(compiled, edited and annotated by Clem Seecharan, 2019)
Inheritance (2020)

Edited
Kyk Over Al – Magazine (1984-2000)
AJS at 70 (1984)
Selected Poems of Martin Carter (1989)
Collected Poems of A.J. Seymour (with J. de Weever, 2000)

Anthology
Heinemann Book Of Caribbean Poetry
(selected by Ian McDonald and Stewart Brown, 1992)
They came in Ships (Guyanese East Indian Writing)
(with Lloyd Searwar, Joel Benjamin, Laxhmie Kallicharran, 1998)
The Bowling Was Super Fine – West Indian Cricket Writing
(with Stewart Brown, 2012)